OLIVIER MESSIAEN

The Untold Story Of A Musical Visionary

Rylan Hartwell

Copyright© 2024 Rylan Hartwell. All rights reserved.

All rights reserved. No part of this book may be reproduced, distributed, or transmitted in any form or by any means, including photocopying, recording, or other electronic or mechanical methods, without the prior written permission of the publisher, except in the case of brief quotations embodied in critical reviews and certain other noncommercial uses permitted by copyright law.

TABLE OF CONTENTS

FOREWORD 5

INTRODUCTION 20

CHAPTER ONE 41

   Childhood And Musical Beginnings 41

CHAPTER TWO 53

   The Paris Conservatoire Years 53

CHAPTER THREE 64

   Stalag VIII-A and "Quatuor pour la fin du temps 64

CHAPTER FOUR 74

   Sacred Sounds And The Organist of La Trinité 74

CHAPTER FIVE 87

   Birdsong and Composition 87

CHAPTER SIX 100

Innovating Musical Language........................ 100

CHAPTER SEVEN... 113

The Marriage of Color and Music............. 113

CHAPTER EIGHT... 126

The Teacher's Podium And Nurturing Future Luminaries... 126

FOREWORD

Visionaries reshape our perception of reality. They challenge established norms, pushing boundaries until the extraordinary becomes conceivable. In the realm of 20th-century music, few figures embody this transformative spirit more profoundly than Olivier Messiaen.

French composer, organist, and ornithologist, Messiaen stood as a colossus astride the tumultuous currents of modernism, his gaze fixed upon horizons invisible to his contemporaries. To understand Messiaen is to embark on a journey through landscapes of sound hitherto unexplored, to witness the birth of new musical languages, and to confront the ineffable through the medium of organized noise.

Conventional story often fail to capture the essence of revolutionary artists. They reduce complex lives to simple trajectories, flattening the peaks and valleys of human experience into digestible anecdotes. "Olivier Messiaen: The Untold Symphony of a Musical Visionary" rejects such reductionism. Instead, it presents a nuanced portrait of a man whose life was as intricate and multifaceted as his compositions.

Messiaen's musical odyssey began in the crucible of early 20th-century France, a nation still reeling from the aftershocks of impressionism and the cataclysm of the Great War. Born in 1908, he came of age in a world where the old certainties had crumbled, and artists of all stripes sought new means of expression. For Messiaen, this quest would lead him down paths untrodden, guided by an unwavering faith and an insatiable curiosity about the natural world.

Critics have often struggled to categorize Messiaen's work, finding it resistant to easy classification. His music defies conventional analysis, incorporating elements as diverse as Gregorian chant, Indian ragas, and the songs of exotic birds. Yet to focus solely on these surface-level influences is to miss the profound originality of his vision. Messiaen did not merely borrow or imitate; he transmuted these disparate elements into something entirely new, a musical language uniquely his own.

Central to understanding Messiaen's artistic journey is his deep Catholic faith. Unlike many of his secular-minded peers, Messiaen embraced spirituality as a wellspring of creativity. His belief in the divine did not constrain his musical explorations but rather expanded them, allowing him to probe the limits of human perception and expression. Works like "Vingt regards sur l'enfant-Jésus" and the opera "Saint François d'Assise" stand as testaments to his ability to render the ineffable in sound, creating aural experiences that transcend mere entertainment to become acts of worship.

Equally crucial to Messiaen's development was his lifelong fascination with birdsong. Far from a mere hobby, his ornithological studies profoundly influenced his compositional techniques. Messiaen viewed birds as nature's greatest musicians, their songs offering a glimpse into a realm of pure, unmediated musical expression. By incorporating these avian melodies into his works, he sought to bridge the gap between human artifice and natural beauty, creating music that resonated with the rhythms of the earth itself.

Innovations in rhythm formed another cornerstone of Messiaen's musical revolution. Rejecting the tyranny of regular meter, he developed complex rhythmic structures inspired by ancient Greek and Hindu sources. These "additive" rhythms, combined with his use of "non-retrogradable" rhythms, created a sense of time suspended, allowing listeners to experience duration in entirely new ways. Messiaen's approach to rhythm was not merely technical innovation for its own sake but a means of expressing his mystical worldview through sound.

Perhaps most striking among Messiaen's contributions to 20th-century music was his exploration of harmony through the lens of synesthesia. For Messiaen, sounds and colors were inextricably linked, each chord evoking specific visual sensations. This unique neurological trait led him to develop his theory of "modes of limited transposition," harmonic structures that produced particular color associations. Through these modes, Messiaen created soundscapes of unprecedented richness and complexity, inviting listeners to experience music not just aurally but visually as well.

Pedagogy played a crucial role in cementing Messiaen's legacy. As a professor at the Paris Conservatoire, he influenced generations of composers, including such luminaries as Pierre Boulez and Karlheinz Stockhausen. His teaching methods, like his compositions, were unconventional and deeply personal. Messiaen encouraged his students to find their own voices, to push beyond the boundaries of tradition, and to seek inspiration in unexpected places. In doing so, he ensured that his revolutionary approach to music would continue to resonate long after his death.

Messiaen's life was not without its trials. His experiences as a prisoner of war during World War II, culminating in the composition of the "Quatuor pour la fin du temps" under the most adverse conditions imaginable, reveal a spirit of indomitable creativity. This seminal work, premiered before an audience of fellow prisoners and guards in Stalag VIII-A, stands as a testament to the power of art to transcend even the darkest of circumstances.

Detractors have accused Messiaen of indulgence, of creating music that is overly complex or esoteric. Such criticisms betray a fundamental misunderstanding of his artistic goals. Messiaen did not compose for easy listening or mass appeal. His music demands active engagement, challenging listeners to expand their perceptions and confront their preconceptions about what music can be. In an age of increasing commodification and homogenization of art, Messiaen's uncompromising vision serves as a vital reminder of music's potential to transform and elevate the human spirit.

"Olivier Messiaen: The Untold Symphony of a Musical Visionary" delves deep into the life and work of this extraordinary figure. It offers readers an unprecedented glimpse into the mind of a genius who reshaped the musical landscape of the 20th century. Through meticulous research and insightful analysis, the author illuminates the myriad influences that shaped Messiaen's artistic development, from his early exposure to the works of Debussy and Stravinsky to his later encounters with non-Western musical traditions.

Readers will discover a Messiaen far more complex and human than the austere figure often presented in music history textbooks. They will encounter a man of profound contradictions: deeply spiritual yet fiercely intellectual, rooted in tradition yet relentlessly innovative. The book explores Messiaen's relationships with his contemporaries, his struggles with ill health and personal tragedy, and the evolution of his musical philosophy over the course of a long and prolific career.

Particular attention is paid to Messiaen's most significant works, offering detailed analyses that reveal the intricate structures and hidden meanings beneath their surface. From the cosmic scale of "Des canyons aux étoiles" to the intimate spirituality of "Visions de l'Amen," each composition is examined in its historical and personal context, providing readers with new insights into Messiaen's creative process.

Musical notation, while necessary for a comprehensive understanding of Messiaen's techniques, can often be daunting for non-specialists. This biography strikes a delicate balance, offering enough technical detail to satisfy scholars while remaining accessible to general readers. Through clear explanations and well-chosen examples, the author demystifies complex concepts like modes of limited transposition and non-retrogradable rhythms, allowing readers to appreciate the full scope of Messiaen's innovations.

Messiaen's influence extends far beyond the realm of classical music. His ideas about sound, color, and time have inspired artists working in diverse fields, from electronic music pioneers to avant-garde filmmakers. This biography traces these connections, demonstrating how Messiaen's revolutionary approach to composition continues to resonate in unexpected ways across the cultural landscape.

Environmental concerns, while not always explicitly stated in Messiaen's work, form a crucial undercurrent in his musical philosophy. His deep connection to the natural world, expressed most vividly through his use of birdsong, takes on new significance in our era of ecological crisis. This biography explores how Messiaen's music can be understood as a call to reconnect with nature, to listen more closely to the symphony of life that surrounds us.

No discussion of Messiaen would be complete without addressing the spiritual dimensions of his work. While his Catholicism is well-documented, this biography goes beyond surface-level analysis to explore the complex interplay between faith and art in Messiaen's life. It examines how his religious beliefs informed his approach to composition, and how, in turn, his musical explorations deepened his spiritual understanding.

Controversies and criticisms are not shied away from. The book addresses the debates surrounding Messiaen's use of serialism, his sometimes difficult relationship with the avant-garde, and the accusations of cultural appropriation leveled at his incorporation of non-

Western musical elements. These issues are examined with nuance and fairness, placing them within the broader context of 20th-century cultural and political tensions.

Messiaen's legacy in the 21st century forms the culmination of this biographical journey. The book examines how contemporary composers, performers, and listeners are engaging with Messiaen's work, discovering new relevance in his ideas about sound and perception. It poses challenging questions about the future of classical music and the role of visionary artists in shaping our cultural discourse.

Ultimately, "Olivier Messiaen: The Untold Symphony of a Musical Visionary" is more than just a biography. It is an invitation to listen differently, to open our ears and minds to new possibilities of musical expression. In exploring the life and work of this extraordinary composer, we are challenged to reconsider our own relationship to sound, time, and the ineffable mysteries of existence.

Messiaen's music continues to provoke, inspire, and transform. It demands of us the courage to confront the unknown, to push beyond the boundaries of convention, and to seek transcendence in the midst of our often chaotic and fragmented world. This biography serves as a guide on that journey, offering readers the tools to engage more deeply with Messiaen's revolutionary vision.

For those willing to undertake this odyssey, the rewards are immeasurable. To immerse oneself in Messiaen's world is to experience music anew, to discover colors in sound, rhythms in nature, and harmonies that resonate with the very fabric of the cosmos. It is to be reminded of art's power to elevate the human spirit and to glimpse, however fleetingly, the infinite possibilities that lie beyond the horizon of our everyday perception.

Olivier Messiaen stands as a beacon of artistic integrity and visionary thinking in an age often characterized by cynicism and superficiality. His life's work challenges us to listen more deeply, to see more clearly, and to engage more fully with the wondrous complexity of our world. This biography does justice to that legacy, offering readers a profound and transformative encounter with one of the true giants of 20th-century music.

Let the journey begin.

INTRODUCTION

Twentieth-century music stands as a labyrinth of innovation, experimentation, and radical reimagining of what sound can be. At its heart, towering above many of his contemporaries, stands Olivier Messiaen composer, organist, ornithologist, synesthete, and visionary. To embark on a study of Messiaen's life and work is to undertake a journey through the very essence of modern classical music, a voyage that challenges preconceptions and expands the boundaries of artistic expression.

Born in 1908 and living until 1992, Messiaen's life spanned nearly the entire 20th century, a period of unprecedented upheaval and transformation. Two world wars, the rise and fall of ideologies, technological revolutions, and seismic shifts in artistic movements all formed the backdrop against which Messiaen composed his revolutionary works. Yet to view him merely as a product of his time would be to grossly underestimate the singular nature of his genius.

Messiaen defied easy categorization. He was at once deeply traditional and radically innovative, a devout Catholic whose music pushed the boundaries of spiritual expression, a Frenchman whose compositions drew inspiration from sources as diverse as Indian ragas and Japanese Noh theater. His work demands a recalibration of our understanding of what music can be and do.

Critics have often struggled to place Messiaen within the conventional narratives of 20th-century music. He stood apart from the serialists, though he experimented with their techniques. He was not strictly an avant-garde figure, yet his innovations were far-reaching and profound. He embraced electronic instruments but remained committed to traditional orchestral forms. In short, Messiaen carved out a unique space in the musical landscape, one that continues to challenge and inspire composers and listeners alike.

Central to understanding Messiaen's artistic vision is his synaesthesia, a neurological condition that caused him to perceive colors when hearing certain musical chords. Far from being a mere curiosity, this trait profoundly influenced his approach to composition. Messiaen developed a complex system of "color chords" and modes of limited transposition, creating music that was as much a visual experience as an auditory one. His work "Couleurs de la Cité Céleste" (Colors of the Celestial City) stands as a testament to this unique sensory fusion, inviting listeners to experience sound in an entirely new dimension.

Messiaen's innovations in rhythm were equally revolutionary. Rejecting the constraints of traditional Western meter, he drew inspiration from ancient Greek and Hindu rhythms, as well as the irregular patterns found in nature. His use of additive rhythms and non-retrogradable rhythms created a sense of time suspended, allowing listeners to experience duration in ways previously unexplored in Western music. Works like "Quartet for the End of Time," composed and first performed while Messiaen was a prisoner of war in a German camp, demonstrate the power of these rhythmic innovations to convey profound emotional and spiritual states.

Nature, particularly birdsong, played a crucial role in Messiaen's compositional process. An avid ornithologist, he spent countless hours in the field, meticulously notating the songs of birds from around the world. These were not mere imitations but complex transcriptions that captured the essence of avian music while translating it into human musical terms. Compositions like "Oiseaux exotiques" (Exotic Birds) and "Catalogue d'oiseaux" (Bird Catalog) represent the culmination of this lifelong passion, blurring the lines between natural and human-made music in ways that continue to astonish and inspire.

Messiaen's Catholic faith was not merely a personal belief but a driving force behind his creative output. Unlike many of his contemporaries who embraced secular or atheistic philosophies, Messiaen saw his music as a means of expressing and exploring divine mysteries. Works such as "Vingt Regards sur l'Enfant-Jésus" (Twenty Contemplations on the Infant Jesus) and the monumental opera "Saint François d'Assise" are not just religious in theme but attempt to embody spiritual experiences through sound. This fusion of the sacred and the avant-garde remains one of the most distinctive and challenging aspects of Messiaen's oeuvre.

Pedagogy formed another crucial dimension of Messiaen's legacy. As a professor at the Paris Conservatoire, he influenced generations of composers, including such luminaries as Pierre Boulez, Karlheinz Stockhausen, and Iannis Xenakis. His teaching methods were as unconventional as his compositions, encouraging students to find inspiration in diverse sources and to push beyond the boundaries of traditional Western music theory. Messiaen's treatise

"Technique de mon langage musical" (Technique of My Musical Language) continues to be a seminal text for composers seeking to understand and build upon his innovations.

Controversy often followed Messiaen's work. His use of birdsong was criticized by some as mere gimmickry, while others found his religious themes at odds with the prevailing secular trends in modern art. His complex rhythms and harmonies were deemed inaccessible by critics who favored more traditional forms. Yet these very elements that drew criticism also cemented Messiaen's place as one of the most original and influential composers of his time. His unwavering commitment to his artistic vision, regardless of prevailing fashions or critical reception, stands as a model of artistic integrity.

Messiaen's influence extends far beyond the realm of classical music. His ideas about the relationship between sound and color have inspired visual artists and filmmakers. His explorations of non-Western rhythms and timbres paved the way for the world music movement of the late 20th century. Even popular music has felt his impact, with progressive rock bands citing his complex rhythms and unconventional harmonies as influences. In an age of increasing cross-pollination between artistic disciplines, Messiaen's multifaceted approach to composition seems more relevant than ever.

Examining Messiaen's life and work inevitably raises profound questions about the nature of music itself. What is the relationship between sound and spirituality? How can music engage with the natural world in meaningful ways? What are the limits of human perception, and how can art push beyond them? These questions, central to Messiaen's artistic quest, continue to resonate with composers, performers, and listeners in the 21st century.

Technological advancements have opened new avenues for exploring Messiaen's ideas. Computer analysis has revealed layers of complexity in his compositions that were not fully appreciated during his lifetime. Electronic and digital instruments offer new possibilities for realizing the timbres and textures Messiaen envisioned. At the same time, ecological concerns have brought renewed attention to his deep engagement with the natural world, particularly his use of birdsong as a bridge between human and animal music-making.

Messiaen's approach to time in music deserves special consideration. His concept of "non-retrogradable rhythms" rhythmic palindromes that sound the same whether played forward or backward challenged linear notions of musical time. In works like "Quatuor pour la fin du temps" (Quartet for the End of Time), Messiaen sought to create a sense of timelessness, reflecting his belief in the eternal nature of divine love. This manipulation of musical time continues to fascinate composers and theorists, offering new ways to think about structure and perception in music.

Cultural appropriation is a thorny issue when discussing Messiaen's work. His incorporation of non-Western musical elements, particularly Indian ragas and rhythms, raises questions about the ethics of cross-cultural borrowing in art.

While Messiaen approached these sources with genuine respect and scholarly interest, contemporary discussions of his work must grapple with the power dynamics inherent in a European composer adopting and transforming non-European musical traditions.

Messiaen's synaesthesia offers a unique entry point into discussions of neurodiversity in the arts. His condition, far from being a hindrance, became a wellspring of creativity. In an era of increasing awareness and appreciation of neurodivergent perspectives, Messiaen's work demonstrates the potential for alternative neurological experiences to enrich and expand artistic expression.

Performance practice of Messiaen's music presents unique challenges. His scores often include detailed instructions about tempo, dynamics, and even the colors he associated with certain passages. Performers must grapple with how to interpret these directions, balancing fidelity to the composer's vision with their own artistic intuitions. This tension between precision and interpretation continues to spark debate among musicians and scholars.

Messiaen's place in the canon of 20th-century music remains a subject of ongoing reassessment. While his importance is widely acknowledged, the full scope of his influence is still being uncovered. As musical cultures around the world continue to intersect and influence each other, Messiaen's multicultural approach to composition seems increasingly prescient. His work offers a model for how composers can engage with diverse traditions while maintaining a distinct artistic voice.

Environmental themes in Messiaen's music have taken on new resonance in the face of global ecological crises. His deep connection to the natural world, expressed most vividly through his use of birdsong, can be seen as a call to attentiveness to the non-human world. In an age of increasing disconnection from nature, Messiaen's music offers a path to reengagement, inviting listeners to tune in to the complex symphonies of the natural environment.

Messiaen's religious faith, so central to his work, poses challenges for secular audiences and performers. How should we approach music that is explicitly conceived as an expression of Catholic theology in an increasingly diverse and secular world? This question goes to the heart of ongoing debates about the relationship between an artist's personal beliefs and the universal appeal of their work.

Digital technologies offer new ways to engage with Messiaen's music. Virtual reality could potentially allow listeners to experience the synesthetic aspects of his compositions, creating immersive environments that combine sound and color as Messiaen himself perceived them. Artificial intelligence analysis of his scores may reveal patterns and structures not previously recognized by human analysts. These technological approaches, while exciting, also raise questions about the nature of musical experience and the role of human interpretation in understanding complex works of art.

Messiaen's life itself reads like a compelling narrative of 20th-century cultural history. From his early studies at the Paris Conservatoire to his imprisonment during World War II, from his groundbreaking teaching career to his late masterpieces, Messiaen's biography offers a unique perspective on the artistic and social transformations of his time. His personal relationships, particularly his marriage to the virtuoso pianist Yvonne Loriod, provide insight into the intimate connections between his life experiences and his creative output.

Accessibility remains a contentious issue in discussions of Messiaen's music. His complex rhythms, unusual harmonies, and often lengthy compositions can be challenging for listeners accustomed to more traditional classical music or popular forms. Yet many argue that the effort required to engage with Messiaen's work is richly rewarded by the depth and originality of his musical vision. This tension between complexity and accessibility continues to be a central issue in contemporary classical music.

Messiaen's focus on timbre the quality or color of musical tones was another revolutionary aspect of his work. His use of unusual instrumental combinations, such as the ondes Martenot in "Turangalîla-Symphonie," expanded the palette of orchestral colors available to composers. This exploration of timbre paved the way for later developments in spectral music and electronic composition, emphasizing the importance of sound quality as a primary compositional parameter.

Legacy of Messiaen extends beyond his own compositions to the work of his students and those influenced by his ideas. Tracing these lines of influence reveals a complex web of musical innovation that spans continents and generations.

From the total serialism of Pierre Boulez to the stochastic music of Iannis Xenakis, from the spectralism of Tristan Murail to the mystic minimalism of Arvo Pärt, Messiaen's impact can be heard in diverse strands of contemporary music.

Questions of national identity in Messiaen's music are complex and sometimes contradictory. While deeply rooted in French musical traditions, his work transcends national boundaries, incorporating influences from around the world. This tension between the local and the global in Messiaen's oeuvre reflects broader questions about cultural identity in an increasingly interconnected world.

Messiaen's approach to musical notation pushed the boundaries of what could be conveyed on the printed page. His scores often include extensive performance notes, unconventional symbols, and even color indications. This expansion of notational possibilities has had lasting impacts on how composers communicate their intentions to performers, leading to ongoing debates about the nature of the musical score and its relationship to performance.

Reception of Messiaen's music has evolved significantly over time. Works that were once considered shocking or inaccessible are now part of the standard repertoire. This shift in perception offers insights into changing attitudes toward modernism in music and the processes by which radical innovations become assimilated into mainstream cultural consciousness.

Philosophical implications of Messiaen's work extend far beyond the realm of music theory. His attempts to represent the infinite and the divine through finite musical means engage with fundamental questions of aesthetics and metaphysics. His music invites us to consider the limits of human perception and expression, and the possibility of transcending those limits through art.

In conclusion, Olivier Messiaen stands as a singular figure in the landscape of 20th-century music, a composer whose work continues to challenge, inspire, and transform our understanding of what music can be. His fusion of spirituality and modernism, his innovative approaches to rhythm, harmony, and timbre, and his profound engagement with the natural world offer rich territory for exploration and interpretation. As we continue to grapple with the complexities of our own time technological, ecological, and spiritual Messiaen's music provides not just a historical artifact but a living resource, a wellspring of ideas and inspirations for artists and thinkers across disciplines.

This biography seeks to illuminate the many facets of Messiaen's life and work, contextualizing his achievements within the broader currents of 20th-century culture while also highlighting the singular nature of his vision. Through detailed analysis of key works, exploration of his philosophical and spiritual ideas, and examination of his lasting influence, we aim to provide readers with a comprehensive understanding of one of the most significant composers of the modern era.

Messiaen's journey from a young prodigy at the Paris Conservatoire to a towering figure in contemporary classical music is a testament to the power of unwavering artistic conviction. His life's work stands as a challenge and an invitation to listen more deeply, to perceive more fully, and to continually expand our understanding of what music can express and achieve. In exploring Messiaen's world, we embark on nothing less than a reimagining of the possibilities of sound itself.

CHAPTER ONE

Childhood And Musical Beginnings

Olivier Eugène Prosper Charles Messiaen was born on December 10, 1908, in Avignon, France, into a family steeped in a rich cultural and intellectual milieu. His father, Pierre Messiaen, was a professor of English and a noted Shakespearean scholar, whose translations of the Bard's works were highly esteemed. His mother, Cécile Sauvage, was a poet whose lyrical verse would profoundly influence her son's artistic sensibilities. This cultured household provided a fertile ground for the young Olivier's burgeoning creativity.

Cécile's poetry, imbued with a deep sense of nature and spirituality, resonated with Olivier from an early age. Her influence is evident in his later works, where themes of nature and mysticism recur. Pierre's scholarly rigor and his dedication to literature also played a significant role, fostering an environment where artistic expression and intellectual exploration were encouraged. The dual influence of his parents created a unique synergy that shaped Olivier's artistic trajectory.

Olivier's early exposure to music was primarily through his mother, who often sang to him and played the piano. These early musical experiences were complemented by the family's relocation to Grenoble in 1914, amidst the backdrop of World War I. In this serene setting, away from the turmoil, Olivier's musical inclinations began to crystallize. His parents' support was unwavering; recognizing their son's prodigious talent, they provided him with a piano and enrolled him in lessons, setting the stage for his future in music.

By the age of seven, Messiaen's musical talents were already evident. He began composing small pieces, displaying a remarkable aptitude for melody and harmony. His formal musical education commenced at the Paris Conservatoire, one of the most prestigious music schools in the world, where he was admitted at the age of 11. Under the tutelage of eminent professors such as Jean Gallon for harmony, Georges Caussade for counterpoint and fugue, and Marcel Dupré for organ, Olivier's musical prowess flourished.

At the Conservatoire, Messiaen's education was rigorous and comprehensive. He studied piano under the guidance of Georges Falkenberg and later Paul Dukas for composition, who became a significant influence on his work. Dukas, a composer known for his exacting standards and innovative techniques, encouraged Messiaen to develop his unique voice. Under Dukas's mentorship, Olivier refined his compositional style, which was characterized by its vivid colors, complex rhythms, and deep spirituality.

Messiaen's first major work, "La Nativité du Seigneur" (The Nativity of the Lord), composed in 1935, is a testament to his early mastery. This nine-movement organ cycle not only showcased his technical prowess but also his ability to infuse music with profound religious and mystical elements. The piece was groundbreaking, combining traditional forms with innovative harmonic structures, and it firmly established Messiaen as a significant figure in the world of classical music.

During these formative years, Messiaen also developed an interest in ornithology, the study of birds, which would later become a significant influence on his music. He began to incorporate birdsong into his compositions, viewing birds as divine messengers whose songs were a form of music that transcended human creation. This fascination with birdsong is evident in many of his later works, where he meticulously transcribed and incorporated the melodies of various bird species.

Messiaen's education was not limited to Western classical traditions. He was deeply influenced by the modal systems of ancient Greek music, Hindu rhythms, and the rich melodic and rhythmic diversity of non-Western cultures. These elements converged in his compositions, creating a distinctive sound that was both innovative and deeply rooted in a sense of universality. His exploration of these diverse musical traditions was part of a broader quest to understand and express the divine through music.

By the end of his education at the Conservatoire, Messiaen had already begun to establish his reputation as a composer of extraordinary talent and originality. His early works demonstrated a bold departure from traditional harmonic and rhythmic conventions, paving the way for his later innovations. The synthesis of his parents' cultural and intellectual influences, his rigorous musical education, and his exploration of diverse musical traditions laid the foundation for his future as one of the most visionary composers of the 20th century.

Religion and nature were central to Messiaen's life and work from a young age. Raised in a devout Catholic household, his faith was a constant source of inspiration and solace. His mother's poetry often reflected a mystical connection with nature, which resonated deeply with him. These themes became intertwined in his music, where he sought to convey the transcendent beauty of the natural world and the divine.

Messiaen's first compositions were often inspired by his religious beliefs. He saw music as a means of expressing the inexpressible, a way to connect with the divine. His early works, such as "Le Banquet Céleste" (The Heavenly Banquet), composed in 1928, reflect this spiritual quest. The piece, which he composed at the age of 20, is characterized by its slow, meditative tempo and rich harmonic textures, evoking a sense of the sacred.

Nature, particularly the landscape around Grenoble where he spent his childhood, also played a crucial role in shaping Messiaen's musical vision. The majestic mountains, serene lakes, and diverse birdlife of the region left an indelible mark on him. He often spoke of the natural world as a reflection of the divine, a source of endless wonder and inspiration. This connection is evident in his music, where the sounds of nature, especially birdsong, are woven into his compositions.

Messiaen's profound love for nature and his deep religious faith were not merely sources of inspiration but were also integral to his identity as an artist. He believed that music had the power to reveal the divine presence in the world, to capture moments of transcendence and awe. This belief guided his compositional process, leading him to create works that were both innovative and deeply spiritual.

Messiaen's early exposure to a wide range of musical traditions and his deep spiritual and intellectual influences coalesced to form a unique musical language. His compositions are characterized by their use of complex rhythms, unconventional harmonic structures, and rich, vibrant colors. He developed a system of "modes of limited transposition," scales that can only be transposed a limited number of times before repeating themselves, which became a hallmark of his style.

These modes, which Messiaen described as "colored," were a way for him to explore the relationship between sound and color. He had a form of synesthesia, a condition where he perceived colors in response to certain musical harmonies. This synesthetic perception profoundly influenced his approach to composition, leading him to create music that was not only heard but also experienced visually.

Messiaen's rhythmic innovations were equally groundbreaking. He was fascinated by the complex rhythms of Indian classical music and the additive rhythms found in ancient Greek poetry. He incorporated these influences into his work, creating rhythmic patterns that were highly intricate and unpredictable. His use of rhythm was not merely technical but also deeply expressive, conveying a sense of movement and energy that was both dynamic and meditative.

By the time he completed his formal education, Messiaen had developed a distinctive compositional voice that set him apart from his contemporaries. His early works demonstrated a bold synthesis of traditional and innovative elements, a willingness to explore new musical territories, and a deep commitment to expressing his spiritual and intellectual vision through music. These qualities would continue to define his work throughout his career, making him one of the most influential and revered composers of the 20th century.

Olivier Messiaen's early years were marked by a rich tapestry of cultural, intellectual, and spiritual influences. His family background and early exposure to music provided a solid foundation for his artistic development. His formal musical education at the Paris Conservatoire honed his technical skills and introduced him to a wide range of musical traditions. The profound impact of his parents' intellectual pursuits, his deep religious faith, and his love of nature converged to shape his unique musical language.

Messiaen's first compositions and his innovative approach to harmony and rhythm established him as a formidable talent in the world of classical music. His ability to synthesize diverse influences into a cohesive and distinctive style set the stage for his future contributions to the musical landscape.

CHAPTER TWO

The Paris Conservatoire Years

Olivier Messiaen entered the Paris Conservatoire in 1919, a prestigious institution renowned for its rigorous musical training. His admission at the age of 11 marked the beginning of an intensive period of study that would shape his future as a composer. During his time at the Conservatoire, Messiaen studied under some of the most eminent musicians of the time, including Paul Dukas and Marcel Dupré, whose guidance and mentorship were instrumental in his development.

Paul Dukas, best known for his orchestral work "The Sorcerer's Apprentice," was a professor of composition at the Conservatoire. Dukas was not only a distinguished composer but also a highly respected teacher known for his meticulous and exacting standards. He encouraged his students to develop their own voices rather than merely imitating established styles. Under Dukas's tutelage, Messiaen learned the importance of structure, form, and the expressive potential of orchestration. Dukas's emphasis on originality and innovation resonated deeply with Messiaen, who was already inclined towards exploring new musical frontiers.

Dukas's influence on Messiaen extended beyond technical instruction. He instilled in his students a profound respect for the traditions of classical music while simultaneously encouraging them to push the boundaries of those traditions. This dual approach was crucial in shaping Messiaen's compositional philosophy. Dukas recognized Messiaen's extraordinary talent and unique vision, providing him with the freedom to experiment and develop his distinctive style. The relationship between teacher and student was one of mutual respect and admiration, fostering an environment where Messiaen could thrive creatively.

Marcel Dupré, another pivotal figure in Messiaen's education, was an acclaimed organist and composer. Dupré's expertise in organ music had a significant impact on Messiaen, who would go on to become one of the most renowned organ composers of the 20th century. Under Dupré's guidance, Messiaen honed his skills in organ performance and improvisation. Dupré's teachings emphasized the importance of technical proficiency and the expressive possibilities of the organ, which resonated with Messiaen's own aspirations.

Dupré's influence is evident in Messiaen's early organ works, such as "Le Banquet Céleste" (1928) and "L'Ascension" (1933-1934), which demonstrate a mastery of the instrument and a deep understanding of its capabilities. These compositions reflect Dupré's emphasis on clarity, precision, and the use of the organ's full range of colors and textures. Messiaen's ability to blend technical mastery with profound expressiveness can be traced back to his studies with Dupré.

The education Messiaen received at the Conservatoire under Dukas and Dupré was comprehensive and rigorous. He studied harmony, counterpoint, and fugue, gaining a thorough grounding in the theoretical aspects of music. This solid foundation allowed him to explore more innovative and unconventional approaches in his compositions. Messiaen's fascination with rhythm, for instance, was partly inspired by his exposure to the complex rhythmic structures in Dukas's and Dupré's works, as well as his own interests in non-Western music traditions.

The Paris Conservatoire was not just a place of learning for Messiaen; it was also a fertile ground for experimentation and discovery. During his years at the Conservatoire, Messiaen began to develop a compositional style that would set him apart from his contemporaries. His unique voice emerged through a synthesis of his rigorous training, personal experiences, and broad intellectual and spiritual interests.

One of the hallmarks of Messiaen's music is his use of "modes of limited transposition," a concept he developed that involves scales that can only be transposed a limited number of times before they repeat themselves. This technique creates a sense of tonal ambiguity and color, which became a signature aspect of his work. The modes allowed Messiaen to explore new harmonic territories, moving away from traditional Western tonality and creating music that was both innovative and deeply expressive.

Messiaen's interest in rhythm also played a crucial role in the development of his style. He was particularly fascinated by the complex rhythms found in non-Western music, especially the rhythms of Indian classical music. He incorporated these rhythms into his compositions, creating intricate and often unpredictable rhythmic patterns. This interest in rhythm was complemented by his studies in ancient Greek rhythms and the poetry of his mother, Cécile Sauvage, whose verse often employed irregular and fluid rhythmic structures.

Another defining characteristic of Messiaen's music is his use of color. He had a form of synesthesia, a neurological condition in which one sensory experience involuntarily triggers another, such as seeing colors in response to music. This synesthetic perception influenced his approach to harmony and orchestration, leading him to describe and compose music in terms of colors. For Messiaen, certain chords and harmonic combinations evoked specific colors, which he then used to shape the emotional and aesthetic impact of his music.

The influence of his spiritual beliefs is also deeply embedded in Messiaen's music. A devout Catholic, Messiaen saw his music as a form of religious expression and a means of connecting with the divine. His compositions often reflect themes of faith, redemption, and the transcendence of the human experience. This spiritual dimension is evident in works like "La Nativité du Seigneur" (1935) and "Les Corps Glorieux" (1939), which combine complex harmonic and rhythmic structures with a profound sense of spiritual contemplation.

Messiaen's early works also reveal his fascination with nature, particularly birdsong. His interest in ornithology led him to meticulously transcribe the songs of various bird species, incorporating these transcriptions into his compositions. Birds became a symbol of divine beauty and freedom in his music, representing the intersection of nature and spirituality. This theme is especially prominent in later works such as "Catalogue d'oiseaux" (1956-

1958), a seven-book series for solo piano that captures the songs and environments of different birds.

The synthesis of these elements modes of limited transposition, complex rhythms, vivid colors, spiritual themes, and nature formed the core of Messiaen's distinctive compositional style. His works from the Conservatoire years, while still in the process of refinement, already display these innovative characteristics. Pieces like "Le Banquet Céleste" and "La Nativité du Seigneur" are early examples of his mature style, demonstrating his ability to blend technical precision with profound emotional and spiritual depth.

As Messiaen continued to develop his voice, he remained committed to pushing the boundaries of musical expression. His time at the Conservatoire provided him with the technical skills and intellectual framework to explore new ideas, while the guidance of mentors like Dukas and Dupré encouraged him to pursue his unique vision. This period of intense study and experimentation was crucial in shaping Messiaen into one of the most original and influential composers of the 20th century.

Olivier Messiaen's years at the Paris Conservatoire were transformative, laying the groundwork for his development into a pioneering composer. Under the mentorship of Paul Dukas and Marcel Dupré, he gained a rigorous and comprehensive musical education that allowed him to explore and refine his distinctive voice. The influence of these mentors, combined with his personal interests and experiences, led to the emergence of a unique compositional style characterized by innovative harmonic and rhythmic structures, vivid use of color, and deep spiritual and natural themes.

During this formative period, Messiaen began to develop the techniques and ideas that would define his work throughout his career. His modes of limited transposition, complex rhythmic patterns, synesthetic approach to harmony, and incorporation of birdsong all contributed to a body of work that was both groundbreaking and deeply expressive.

CHAPTER THREE

Stalag VIII-A and "Quatuor pour la fin du temps

Olivier Messiaen's experiences as a prisoner of war during World War II were pivotal in shaping one of his most significant works, "Quatuor pour la fin du temps" ("Quartet for the End of Time"). The circumstances surrounding its composition are a testament to Messiaen's resilience, creativity, and unwavering faith, which allowed him to create a masterpiece under the most harrowing conditions.

In 1940, during the early stages of World War II, Messiaen was conscripted into the French army as a medical auxiliary. Despite his pacifist tendencies, he fulfilled his duty and was captured by the German army during the Battle of France.

Messiaen, along with thousands of other French soldiers, was taken prisoner and transported to Stalag VIII-A, a German prisoner-of-war camp located in Görlitz, now part of modern-day Poland.

The conditions at Stalag VIII-A were grim. The camp was overcrowded, and prisoners faced harsh treatment, insufficient food, and inadequate medical care. The winters were particularly brutal, with freezing temperatures and limited shelter. Despite these hardships, the prisoners found ways to maintain their morale and sense of humanity. For Messiaen, this meant turning to his music.

Messiaen's faith was a crucial source of strength during his imprisonment. A devout Catholic, he saw his ordeal as a test of his spiritual resilience and an opportunity to deepen his connection with

God. He found solace in prayer and religious reflection, drawing inspiration from the Book of Revelation, which would later influence the themes of "Quatuor pour la fin du temps.

In the camp, Messiaen encountered fellow musicians: cellist Étienne Pasquier, clarinetist Henri Akoka, and violinist Jean le Boulaire. Recognizing the unique opportunity to create music even in captivity, Messiaen began to compose a piece that would make use of their available instruments. Despite the lack of proper materials and instruments, Messiaen's indomitable spirit and the support of his fellow musicians enabled him to begin work on what would become one of his most renowned compositions.

The environment of the camp, although oppressive, also provided a unique form of inspiration for Messiaen. The daily struggle for survival and the camaraderie among prisoners created a backdrop against which his creative process flourished. He saw music as a means to transcend the physical and emotional confines of the camp, offering both him and his fellow prisoners a sense of hope and spiritual elevation.

"Quatuor pour la fin du temps" is an extraordinary piece not only for its musical innovation but also for the remarkable circumstances of its creation and premiere. Messiaen composed the quartet between 1940 and 1941, amidst the bleak and challenging conditions of Stalag VIII-A. The work is deeply imbued with his religious faith, reflecting his vision of the Apocalypse and the eternity beyond time, as described in the Book of Revelation.

The quartet is written for an unusual combination of instruments: piano, clarinet, violin, and cello. This choice was dictated by the availability of musicians and instruments in the camp. Despite these constraints, Messiaen's composition is a testament to his ingenuity and ability to adapt to his circumstances. Each instrument plays a crucial role in the quartet, contributing to its rich and complex textures.

The piece consists of eight movements, each with a distinct character and purpose, yet all unified by Messiaen's overarching theme of transcending time and earthly suffering. The opening movement, "Liturgie de cristal" ("Crystal Liturgy"), sets the tone for the entire work with its ethereal and otherworldly sound. The movement features the clarinet and violin imitating birdsong, a recurring motif in

Messiaen's music, symbolizing the freedom and beauty of nature even amidst human suffering.

One of the most striking movements is "Louange à l'Éternité de Jésus" ("Praise to the Eternity of Jesus"), a duet for cello and piano. This movement is a slow, meditative piece that expresses profound reverence and devotion. The cello's long, lyrical lines are supported by the piano's gentle chords, creating a sense of timelessness and spiritual contemplation. Messiaen intended this movement to evoke the eternal nature of Christ, offering a moment of solace and reflection in the midst of the quartet's more tumultuous sections.

The movement "Danse de la fureur, pour les sept trompettes" ("Dance of Fury, for the Seven Trumpets") stands out for its rhythmic intensity and dynamic energy. All four instruments play in unison, creating a powerful and dramatic effect. This movement represents the apocalyptic imagery of the seven trumpets from the Book of Revelation, conveying a sense of urgency and divine power.

The quartet concludes with "Louange à l'Immortalité de Jésus" ("Praise to the Immortality of Jesus"), another slow, contemplative piece for violin and piano. This final movement mirrors the earlier "Louange à l'Éternité de Jésus" but with a different instrumental pairing, bringing the work to a serene and spiritually uplifting conclusion.

The premiere of "Quatuor pour la fin du temps" took place on January 15, 1941, in Stalag VIII-A. The performance conditions were far from ideal: the weather was bitterly cold, the instruments were in poor condition, and the audience consisted of fellow prisoners and German guards. Despite these challenges, the premiere was a profound and moving event. The audience, many of whom were experiencing the horrors of war and captivity, found solace and transcendence in Messiaen's music.

Messiaen himself played the piano, with Akoka on clarinet, Pasquier on cello, and Le Boulaire on violin. The performance was a testament to the resilience of the human spirit and the power of music to uplift and inspire even in the darkest of times. The quartet's themes of eternity, divine love, and spiritual transcendence resonated deeply with those who heard it, providing a moment of grace and beauty in the midst of their suffering.

The composition and premiere of "Quatuor pour la fin du temps" had a lasting impact on

Messiaen's career and legacy. The work was quickly recognized as a masterpiece, showcasing his unique compositional voice and his ability to create profound and innovative music under extreme circumstances. It remains one of the most significant and frequently performed pieces of 20th-century chamber music.

"Quatuor pour la fin du temps" is a reflection of Messiaen's unwavering faith and his belief in the transformative power of music. The quartet's creation and performance in Stalag VIII-A are a testament to his resilience and creativity, demonstrating how art can provide hope and meaning even in the most dire situations. The work stands as a beacon of spiritual and artistic triumph, illustrating the profound impact of Messiaen's experiences as a prisoner of war on his music and his life.

Olivier Messiaen's time as a prisoner of war at Stalag VIII-A was a period of immense hardship and challenge, but it also became a fertile ground for his creativity. The composition and premiere of "Quatuor pour la fin du temps" are remarkable achievements that highlight his resilience, faith, and extraordinary talent.

CHAPTER FOUR

Sacred Sounds And The Organist of La Trinité

Olivier Messiaen's appointment as the principal organist at the Church of La Trinité in Paris marked a significant chapter in his life and career. This position, which he held for more than six decades, deeply influenced his music and spiritual journey, allowing him to merge his profound faith with his extraordinary musical talent.

In 1931, at the age of 22, Messiaen was appointed as the organist of La Trinité, a prominent church in the heart of Paris. This position was not only a prestigious one but also a role that came with immense responsibility and visibility. La Trinité, known for its magnificent architecture and rich musical tradition, provided an ideal setting for Messiaen to develop and express his unique artistic vision.

The organ at La Trinité was a remarkable instrument, known for its rich tonal palette and versatility. Designed by Aristide Cavaillé-Coll, one of the most renowned organ builders of the 19th century, the instrument had a profound impact on Messiaen's compositional style. The organ's capabilities allowed him to experiment with a wide range of sounds and textures, contributing to the development of his distinctive musical language.

Messiaen's tenure at La Trinité began at a time when he was already establishing himself as a significant figure in the Parisian music scene. His early compositions, such as "Le banquet céleste" (1928) and "L'ascension" (1932-33), had already garnered attention for their innovative use of harmony and rhythm. However, it was his work at La Trinité that provided the platform for him to refine and expand his musical ideas.

As the principal organist, Messiaen was responsible for performing at Sunday masses, special liturgical services, and numerous other church functions. This role required a deep understanding of liturgical music and an ability to improvise during services, skills in which Messiaen excelled. His improvisations at La Trinité became legendary, often drawing large audiences who came specifically to hear his unique and spiritually uplifting performances.

One of the most significant aspects of Messiaen's work at La Trinité was his ability to fuse his deep religious convictions with his musical creations. His compositions and improvisations were not merely exercises in musical technique but were imbued with his profound spirituality. For Messiaen, music was a means of expressing the divine and exploring the mysteries of faith.

Messiaen's spirituality was the cornerstone of his life and work. A devout Catholic, he viewed his music as a form of religious expression and a way to communicate his faith. His belief in the transcendent power of music was evident in his compositions, many of which were inspired by religious themes and texts.

One of the earliest examples of Messiaen's integration of spirituality and music is "La Nativité du Seigneur" (1935), a cycle of nine meditations for organ. Composed shortly after he began his tenure at La Trinité, this work reflects his deep devotion and theological insights. Each movement of "La Nativité du Seigneur" depicts a different aspect of the Nativity story, using intricate harmonic and rhythmic structures to convey the profound mystery and joy of Christ's birth.

Messiaen's exploration of religious themes continued throughout his career, with many of his major works inspired by his faith. "Les Corps glorieux" (1939), another significant organ work, explores the theme of resurrection and the glorified bodies of the saints. This piece, like many of his compositions, is characterized by its rich harmonic language and use of rhythmic modes, reflecting Messiaen's fascination with the transcendent and eternal.

One of Messiaen's most ambitious and spiritually profound works is "Vingt regards sur l'Enfant-Jésus" (1944), a cycle of twenty pieces for solo piano. This work, composed during the final years of World War II, is a meditation on the infancy of Jesus, exploring various perspectives on the divine child. Each piece in the cycle is marked by its complexity and depth, combining intricate rhythms, innovative harmonies, and thematic symbolism to convey a sense of wonder and reverence.

Messiaen's interest in birdsong, which became a hallmark of his style, also has spiritual roots. He regarded birds as symbols of divine beauty and freedom, seeing their songs as a form of natural music that transcends human creation. This fascination led to the inclusion of transcribed birdsong in many of his works, adding a unique dimension to his musical language. For Messiaen, the songs of birds represented a pure, untainted form of praise to God.

In his monumental work "Catalogue d'oiseaux" (1956-58), Messiaen composed thirteen pieces for solo piano, each depicting the song of a different bird species. This collection not only showcases his technical skill in transcribing birdsong but also reflects his belief in the sacredness of nature. Messiaen's detailed and vivid musical descriptions of birdsong are imbued with a sense of awe and reverence, emphasizing his view of nature as a divine creation.

Another significant aspect of Messiaen's spirituality was his interest in the concept of time and eternity. This theme is evident in many of his compositions, where he sought to express the timeless and infinite nature of the divine. His use of non-retrogradable rhythms (palindromic rhythmic patterns) and modes of limited transposition are examples of his attempt to break away from traditional concepts of musical time, creating a sense of timelessness and transcendence in his music.

Messiaen's fascination with the Apocalypse and the end of time is perhaps most famously expressed in his "Quatuor pour la fin du temps" (1940-41), composed during his imprisonment in Stalag VIII-A. This work, inspired by the Book of Revelation, explores themes of divine judgment, resurrection, and the eternal nature of Christ. The quartet's innovative use of rhythm and harmony, combined with its profound spiritual themes, make it one of Messiaen's most celebrated and influential compositions.

Throughout his career, Messiaen continued to explore the intersection of faith and music, creating works that were both deeply personal and universally resonant. His "Trois petites liturgies de la Présence Divine" (1943-44), for example, is a vibrant and ecstatic celebration of the divine presence, combining voices, orchestra, and electronic instruments to create a rich tapestry of sound. This work, like many of Messiaen's compositions, reflects his belief in the transformative power of music and its ability to convey the divine.

Messiaen's tenure at La Trinité also provided him with a stable and supportive environment in which to develop his pedagogical skills. In addition to his work as a composer and performer, he became a highly respected teacher, influencing a generation of musicians and composers. His students included notable figures such as Pierre Boulez, Karlheinz Stockhausen, and Iannis Xenakis, who would go on to become significant contributors to the world of contemporary music.

Messiaen's teaching was characterized by his emphasis on the importance of rhythm, color, and spirituality in music. He encouraged his students to explore these elements in their own work, fostering a spirit of innovation and experimentation. His influence as a teacher extended beyond the technical aspects of composition, inspiring his students to seek deeper meaning and expression in their music.

One of the defining features of Messiaen's work was his ability to integrate his deep religious faith with innovative musical techniques. This synthesis is evident in his use of what he called "modes of limited transposition" scales that could only be transposed a limited number of times before repeating the same notes. These modes, which he developed and systematized, provided a harmonic language that was both unique and richly expressive.

Messiaen's rhythmic innovations were equally significant. He drew on a wide range of sources, including ancient Greek and Hindu rhythms, to develop complex and non-traditional rhythmic structures. These rhythms, often characterized by irregular and additive patterns, contributed to the otherworldly and timeless quality of his music. For Messiaen, rhythm was not just a structural element but a means of conveying the divine and the eternal.

His fascination with color was another important aspect of his music. Messiaen had a form of synesthesia, a condition in which he experienced specific colors in response to certain musical chords and sounds. This sensory experience influenced his compositional process, leading him to create music that was both aurally and visually rich. His use of coloristic harmonies and orchestration techniques added a unique dimension to his work, making it vividly expressive and evocative.

Messiaen's interest in integrating different art forms is also evident in his "Saint François d'Assise" (1975-83), an opera that combines music, theater, and visual elements to tell the story of St. Francis of Assisi. This work reflects his deep admiration for St. Francis, whom he saw as a model of humility and divine love. The opera's rich and complex score, combined with its spiritual themes, makes it one of Messiaen's most ambitious and significant works.

Throughout his career, Messiaen's work at La Trinité remained a central and grounding aspect of his life. The church provided him with a space to explore and develop his musical ideas, as well as a community that supported and appreciated his work. His role as an organist was not just a job but a vocation, allowing him to live out his faith through his music.

CHAPTER FIVE

Birdsong and Composition

Olivier Messiaen's fascination with birds and their songs was not merely a hobby but a profound influence that shaped his musical oeuvre. His passion for ornithology permeated his compositions, leading to some of the most unique and innovative works in the classical music repertoire. This chapter explores how Messiaen's love for birdsong intertwined with his musical creativity, resulting in a distinctive fusion of natural soundscapes and complex musical structures.

Messiaen's interest in birds began in his childhood. Growing up in the rural countryside of Avignon and later Grenoble, he was surrounded by nature. The sounds of birds were a constant presence in his early life, and he developed a keen ear for their songs. This early exposure to the natural world fostered a deep appreciation for the beauty and complexity of birdsong, which he would carry with him throughout his life.

As a young man, Messiaen's passion for ornithology grew alongside his musical career. He often went on bird-watching excursions, meticulously recording and transcribing the songs he heard. This practice required not only a keen ear but also a deep understanding of musical notation, as he sought to capture the exact pitches, rhythms, and timbres of the birds' calls. His notebooks from these excursions are filled with detailed annotations, reflecting his dedication to accurately preserving the natural sounds he encountered.

Messiaen's approach to birdsong was scientific as well as artistic. He collaborated with ornithologists to deepen his understanding of bird behavior and communication. This collaboration was particularly evident in his work with Jacques Delamain, a renowned French ornithologist. Delamain's influence helped Messiaen refine his techniques for transcribing birdsong, providing him with the knowledge needed to replicate the intricate patterns and structures of avian music.

The impact of birdsong on Messiaen's music is evident in many of his compositions. One of the earliest and most significant examples is the "Catalogue d'oiseaux" (1956-58), a monumental work for solo piano. Comprising thirteen pieces, each dedicated to a different bird species, the "Catalogue d'oiseaux" showcases Messiaen's meticulous transcription of birdsong and his ability to integrate these natural sounds into a cohesive musical framework. Each piece in the collection is a vivid portrayal of the bird's song and its habitat, combining detailed musical notation with evocative descriptions of the natural environment.

Messiaen's use of birdsong was not limited to piano music. He incorporated avian sounds into many of his orchestral and chamber works, using a variety of techniques to blend these natural elements with his complex harmonic and rhythmic language. In "Réveil des oiseaux" (1953), an orchestral work that captures the dawn chorus of birds, Messiaen employs a rich palette of instrumental colors to evoke the diverse sounds of different species. The piece is a celebration of nature's awakening, filled with the vibrant and varied calls of birds greeting the morning.

One of the most ambitious and comprehensive explorations of birdsong in Messiaen's work is "Des Canyons aux étoiles" (1971-74), a twelve-movement composition for piano, horn, xylorimba, glockenspiel, and orchestra. This piece, inspired by the landscapes and wildlife of the American Southwest, integrates birdsong from various species into its intricate musical fabric. Messiaen's ability to seamlessly blend these natural sounds with his innovative compositional techniques is a testament to his skill and creativity.

Messiaen developed a range of techniques to incorporate birdsong into his compositions, creating a unique and recognizable musical language. His methods were both precise and imaginative, allowing him to capture the essence of birdsong while transforming it into a distinctively Messiaenic sound.

One of the fundamental techniques Messiaen used was direct transcription. He meticulously notated the pitches, rhythms, and timbres of birds' calls, often spending hours in the field listening and recording their songs. These transcriptions were then incorporated into his compositions, either as direct quotations or as the basis for more elaborate musical development. In pieces like "La Fauvette des jardins" (1970), a solo piano work dedicated to the garden warbler, Messiaen's transcriptions are presented with remarkable fidelity, capturing the intricate details of the bird's song.

Messiaen's transcriptions were not mere imitations; he adapted them to fit the broader context of his compositions. This adaptation involved transposing the pitches to suit the range of the instrument, adjusting rhythms to align with his complex metrical structures, and orchestrating the birdsong to blend seamlessly with other musical elements. In doing so, he created a dialogue between the natural world and his own musical imagination, resulting in works that are both rooted in reality and transcendently abstract.

In addition to direct transcription, Messiaen employed a technique he called "modes of limited transposition." These modes, which are scales that can only be transposed a limited number of times before repeating the same notes, provided a harmonic framework that echoed the repetitive and cyclical nature of birdsong. By using these modes, Messiaen created a sense of stasis and timelessness in his music, mirroring the eternal and unchanging quality of the natural world. This technique is evident in works like "Oiseaux exotiques" (1955-56), where the harmonic language is deeply influenced by the modal structures derived from birdsong.

Rhythm played a crucial role in Messiaen's incorporation of birdsong. He developed a system of "added values" and "non-retrogradable rhythms" to capture the irregular and complex rhythms of birds' calls. Added values involve the insertion of extra beats or subdivisions into a rhythmic pattern, creating a sense of unpredictability and fluidity. Non-retrogradable rhythms are palindromic patterns that read the same forwards and backwards, embodying the idea of temporal symmetry and eternal recurrence. These rhythmic techniques allowed Messiaen to emulate the spontaneous and varied nature of birdsong, adding a dynamic and organic quality to his music.

Messiaen's use of timbre and orchestration was another key aspect of his approach to birdsong. He employed a wide range of instrumental colors to evoke the diverse sounds of different bird species. In "Éclairs sur l'Au-Delà" (1987-91), his last completed work, Messiaen uses an expansive orchestra to create a vibrant and shimmering soundscape, filled with the calls of birds from around the world. The intricate layering of timbres and the imaginative use of orchestral textures in this piece exemplify his ability to translate the natural soundscape into a rich and immersive musical experience.

Electronics and unconventional instruments also played a role in Messiaen's depiction of birdsong. In "Saint François d'Assise" (1975-83), his opera on the life of St. Francis, Messiaen uses the ondes Martenot, an early electronic instrument, to create ethereal and otherworldly sounds that represent the birds' voices. This use of electronics adds a new dimension to his music, enhancing the sense of mystery and transcendence that characterizes his work.

Messiaen's approach to birdsong was not just about replication but transformation. He saw birds as messengers of the divine, their songs as natural hymns of praise. This spiritual perspective is reflected in his music, where birdsong becomes a means of expressing the ineffable and the eternal. In "La Transfiguration de Notre Seigneur Jésus-Christ" (1965-69), a large-scale oratorio, Messiaen incorporates birdsong to symbolize the divine presence, using their calls to evoke a sense of awe and reverence.

The incorporation of birdsong in Messiaen's music also had a broader philosophical and ecological dimension. He viewed the natural world as a source of inspiration and a reflection of the divine order. His music celebrates the beauty and complexity of nature, inviting listeners to appreciate and contemplate the wonders of the natural world. This ecological awareness is particularly evident in works like "Des Canyons aux étoiles...", where the depiction of birds and landscapes is intertwined with a message of conservation and respect for nature.

Messiaen's use of birdsong extended beyond mere imitation; he often used it as a source of thematic material for his compositions. This thematic integration allowed him to create complex and cohesive musical structures that were deeply rooted in the natural world. In

"Chronochromie" (1959-60), for example, Messiaen uses birdsong as the primary thematic material, developing it through intricate contrapuntal techniques and rich harmonic textures. The result is a work that is both structurally rigorous and vividly evocative of the natural soundscape.

In "La Fauvette passerinette" (1961), a piano piece that remained unpublished during his lifetime, Messiaen constructs the entire composition around the song of the subalpine warbler. The bird's call is not just a decorative element but the foundation of the work's melodic and harmonic structure. This approach demonstrates Messiaen's ability to integrate birdsong into the very fabric of his music, creating compositions that are both innovative and deeply connected to the natural world.

Messiaen's thematic use of birdsong also had a symbolic dimension. He often associated specific birds with particular spiritual or philosophical ideas, using their songs to convey deeper meanings. In "Catalogue d'oiseaux", each bird is not just a source of musical material but a symbol of a particular aspect of nature or spirituality. The golden oriole, for example, represents the joy and brilliance of creation, while the blackbird symbolizes the mystery and depth of the natural world. These symbolic associations add a layer of meaning to Messiaen's music, enriching the listener's experience and understanding.

CHAPTER SIX

Innovating Musical Language

Olivier Messiaen's contribution to the world of music is unparalleled, particularly through his development and use of the "modes of limited transposition." These modes became a cornerstone of his musical language, influencing his harmonic and melodic structures and setting him apart as one of the most innovative composers of the 20th century.

Messiaen's modes of limited transposition are scales that can be transposed only a few times before repeating the same set of pitches. This concept breaks away from the traditional major and minor scales, offering a fresh palette of harmonic possibilities. Messiaen discovered these modes early in his career, and they became a hallmark of his compositional style.

The first mode of limited transposition is the whole-tone scale, consisting of six notes separated by whole steps. This scale can only be transposed once before the original set of notes is repeated. Messiaen's use of the whole-tone scale is evident in many of his early works, providing an otherworldly, floating quality to the music. The lack of leading tones and traditional harmonic resolution in the whole-tone scale creates a sense of stasis, which Messiaen used to evoke timelessness and the infinite.

The second mode, known as the octatonic scale or diminished scale, alternates whole and half steps. This eight-note scale can be transposed only twice before repeating itself. The octatonic scale's unique intervallic structure allows for the creation of complex harmonies and dissonances, which Messiaen exploited to great effect. The octatonic scale features prominently in works such as "Quatuor pour la fin du temps" (Quartet for the End of Time), where it contributes to the mystical and apocalyptic atmosphere of the piece.

The third mode of limited transposition is less commonly used but is equally distinctive. This mode consists of a repeating pattern of half steps and minor thirds, resulting in a nine-note scale. The third mode can be transposed only three times before repeating. Messiaen employed this mode to explore novel harmonic textures and to further expand his musical vocabulary.

Messiaen's fascination with these modes extended beyond their theoretical implications; he integrated them into the very fabric of his compositions. In "Turangalîla-Symphonie" (1946-48), one of his most ambitious works, the modes of limited transposition form the basis of the harmonic language. The symphony's lush, exotic sonorities and rhythmic vitality owe much to Messiaen's innovative use of these scales.

The modes of limited transposition also allowed Messiaen to create a sense of unity and coherence within his works. By restricting the number of transpositions, he established a distinct harmonic identity that pervades each composition. This technique is particularly evident in "Vingt Regards sur l'Enfant-Jésus" (Twenty Contemplations on the Infant Jesus), a monumental piano cycle that explores various aspects of the Nativity story. The recurring use of specific modes helps to bind the work together, creating a cohesive and immersive musical journey.

Messiaen's exploration of the modes of limited transposition was not limited to harmonic innovation; it also influenced his melodic writing. By utilizing these scales, he crafted melodies that are both strikingly original and deeply expressive. The unusual intervallic structures of the modes lend a unique character to Messiaen's melodies, which often possess an otherworldly, transcendent quality. In "Les offrandes oubliées" (The Forgotten Offerings), an early orchestral work, the use of these modes infuses the melodic lines with a sense of mystery and longing.

In addition to his groundbreaking work with modes of limited transposition, Messiaen made significant contributions to the field of rhythm. His exploration of complex rhythms and time structures added another layer of innovation to his music, challenging conventional notions of meter and pulse.

Messiaen's interest in rhythm was deeply rooted in his fascination with non-Western musical traditions, particularly Indian classical music. He was captivated by the intricate rhythmic patterns, or "tālas," used in Indian music and sought to incorporate similar complexity into his own compositions. This interest led to the development of what he called "added values" and "non-retrogradable rhythms."

Added values involve the insertion of an extra rhythmic unit such as a short note or rest into a regular rhythmic pattern. This technique disrupts the regularity of the meter, creating irregular and unpredictable rhythms. Messiaen used added values to infuse his music with a sense of spontaneity and fluidity. In "Livre d'orgue"

(Book of Organ), a collection of organ pieces, he employs added values extensively, resulting in a rhythmic landscape that is both intricate and dynamic.

Non-retrogradable rhythms are palindromic rhythmic patterns that read the same forwards and backwards. These rhythms create a sense of symmetry and balance, reflecting Messiaen's interest in the eternal and the unchanging. Non-retrogradable rhythms are a prominent feature of "Mode de valeurs et d'intensités" (Mode of Durations and Intensities), a piano piece that represents one of Messiaen's earliest forays into total serialism. In this work, rhythmic patterns, pitches, dynamics, and articulations are all subjected to serial procedures, resulting in a composition that is highly structured yet remarkably expressive.

Messiaen's exploration of rhythm extended to his use of "rhythmic cells" small, repeating rhythmic motifs that form the building blocks of his compositions. These cells are often combined and manipulated to create complex, layered rhythms. In "La Nativité du Seigneur" (The Nativity of the Lord), a set of nine organ meditations, Messiaen uses rhythmic cells to generate intricate, overlapping textures that evoke the mystery and wonder of the Nativity story.

One of the most striking examples of Messiaen's rhythmic innovation is found in "Quartet for the End of Time," composed during his internment in a German prisoner-of-war camp during World War II. The work's rhythmic complexity is exemplified in the movement titled "Dance of Fury, for the Seven Trumpets." This movement features relentless, driving rhythms that create a sense of urgency and intensity. The use of rhythmic cells, added values, and non-retrogradable rhythms contributes to the movement's powerful and unsettling character.

Messiaen's approach to rhythm was not limited to small-scale patterns; he also experimented with large-scale rhythmic structures. He often employed irregular and asymmetrical meters, such as 5/8, 7/8, and 11/8, to create a sense of unpredictability and fluidity. In "Chronochromie," a large orchestral work, Messiaen uses these irregular meters to generate complex, shifting rhythms that challenge the listener's perception of time.

Another important aspect of Messiaen's rhythmic language is his use of "metrical modulation," a technique that involves shifting from one meter to another by changing the subdivision of the beat. This technique allows for seamless transitions between different rhythmic patterns and meters, creating a fluid and dynamic sense of time. In "Saint François d'Assise," his only opera, metrical modulation is used to great effect, enhancing the dramatic and narrative flow of the music.

Messiaen's fascination with rhythm was also influenced by his deep Catholic faith. He saw rhythm as a reflection of the divine order, a manifestation of the eternal and the infinite. This spiritual perspective is evident in "La Transfiguration de Notre Seigneur Jésus-Christ" (The Transfiguration of Our Lord Jesus Christ), an oratorio that explores the theme of Christ's transfiguration. The work's complex rhythms and time structures are designed to evoke a sense of the divine, transcending the temporal and reaching towards the eternal.

In "Des canyons aux étoiles" (From the Canyons to the Stars), a large-scale orchestral work inspired by the landscapes of the American Southwest, Messiaen combines his innovative use of rhythm with his love of birdsong and nature. The piece features intricate, overlapping rhythms that evoke the natural world, from the rustling of leaves to the calls of birds. Messiaen's use of rhythm in this work is both descriptive and symbolic, reflecting his belief in the interconnectedness of all creation.

Messiaen's rhythmic innovations had a profound impact on the development of contemporary music. His techniques have been adopted and expanded upon by many composers, influencing a wide range of musical styles and genres.

Composers such as Pierre Boulez, Karlheinz Stockhausen, and George Benjamin have all acknowledged Messiaen's influence on their work, particularly in the realm of rhythm.

In addition to his work as a composer, Messiaen was a dedicated teacher who passed on his rhythmic innovations to a new generation of musicians. As a professor at the Paris Conservatoire, he taught many of the leading composers of the late 20th and early 21st centuries, including Pierre Boulez, Iannis Xenakis, and Gérard Grisey. Through his teaching, Messiaen's ideas about rhythm and time structures have continued to inspire and challenge musicians around the world.

Messiaen's exploration of rhythm was not confined to his notated compositions; it also extended to his performances as an organist. His improvisations at the Church of La Trinité in Paris were renowned for their rhythmic complexity and inventiveness. These improvisations provided a laboratory for Messiaen to experiment with new rhythmic ideas and techniques, many of which found their way into his written works.

CHAPTER SEVEN

The Marriage of Color and Music

Olivier Messiaen's synesthesia was a fundamental aspect of his creative process, deeply influencing his compositions and his perception of music. Synesthesia, a condition in which one sensory experience involuntarily triggers another, allowed Messiaen to perceive sounds as colors. This unique sensory crossover provided him with a rich, multisensory palette from which he drew his musical ideas.

Messiaen's synesthesia was not a mere curiosity; it shaped his entire approach to music. He often described how different chords, scales, and rhythms evoked specific colors and visual patterns. For him, composing music was akin to painting with sound, and each note or chord had a corresponding hue and texture. This perception was not just abstract but vividly concrete, influencing his compositional choices and his understanding of musical structure.

In his writings and interviews, Messiaen detailed how his synesthetic experiences guided his work. For instance, he described the key of E major as a vivid blue, while the whole-tone scale appeared as a shimmering white. These color associations were integral to his compositions, providing a framework for his harmonic language. Messiaen's synesthesia allowed him to create music that was not only sonically rich but also visually evocative, aiming to engage the listener's imagination on multiple sensory levels.

One of the most distinctive elements of Messiaen's music is his use of "color chords." These are harmonies specifically chosen and constructed to evoke particular colors and visual sensations. The creation of color chords was a direct outgrowth of Messiaen's synesthesia, allowing him to translate his visual experiences into musical form.

Messiaen's color chords are characterized by their complex, often unconventional structures. He frequently used extended harmonies and unusual interval combinations to achieve the desired color effects. These chords often defy traditional harmonic progression, instead existing to create a specific sensory impression. In works like "Turangalîla-Symphonie," these color chords are used extensively to generate a kaleidoscopic array of sonic and visual impressions.

A prime example of Messiaen's use of color chords can be found in his piano cycle "Vingt Regards sur l'Enfant-Jésus" (Twenty

Contemplations on the Infant Jesus). In this work, each piece is imbued with a rich tapestry of harmonic colors, reflecting the various aspects of the Nativity story. The ninth movement, "Regard du temps" (Contemplation of Time), employs shimmering, iridescent chords to evoke the timeless, eternal nature of Christ's birth. These chords, with their intricate layers and shifting tonalities, create a sense of awe and wonder, transporting the listener into a realm of divine mystery.

Messiaen's use of color chords was also a way to communicate his deep Catholic faith. He often spoke of music as a means of spiritual expression, and his color chords were a way to convey the ineffable beauty and majesty of the divine. In "La Transfiguration de Notre Seigneur Jésus-Christ" (The Transfiguration of Our Lord Jesus Christ),

Messiaen uses a palette of radiant harmonies to depict the moment of Christ's transfiguration. The chords shimmer and glow, reflecting the heavenly light that envelops Christ and his disciples.

In addition to his religious works, Messiaen's secular compositions also showcase his mastery of color chords. In "Des canyons aux étoiles" (From the Canyons to the Stars.), inspired by the landscapes of the American Southwest, Messiaen uses vibrant, shifting harmonies to evoke the vast, colorful vistas of the canyons. The music captures the play of light and shadow, the deep reds and oranges of the rocks, and the brilliant blues of the sky, creating an auditory painting of the natural world.

Messiaen's exploration of color chords was not limited to static harmonic effects; he also used them to shape the form and structure of his compositions. In "Chronochromie," a large orchestral work, the shifting color chords help to delineate the different sections of the piece, creating a sense of progression and transformation. The music moves through a series of harmonic landscapes, each defined by its unique color palette, leading the listener on a journey through time and space.

Another significant aspect of Messiaen's color chords is their role in his rhythmically complex works. In pieces like "Quatuor pour la fin du temps" (Quartet for the End of Time), the interplay of rhythm and harmony is essential to the overall effect. The color chords, with their rich, overlapping textures, interact with the intricate rhythms to create a sense of timelessness and suspension. This combination of rhythm and color is particularly evident in the fifth movement, "Louange à l'Éternité de Jésus" (Praise to the Eternity of Jesus), where the slow, stately chords and the flowing, meditative rhythm evoke a vision of eternal peace and serenity.

Messiaen's use of color chords also extended to his organ music, where the instrument's wide range of timbres and dynamic possibilities allowed him to fully realize his synesthetic visions. In "Livre d'orgue" (Book of Organ), a collection of organ pieces, Messiaen explores the full spectrum of harmonic color, using the organ's different stops and registrations to create a kaleidoscope of sound. Each piece in the collection is a study in harmonic color, showcasing Messiaen's ability to blend and juxtapose different chords to achieve his desired effects.

In his teaching at the Paris Conservatoire, Messiaen passed on his ideas about color chords to a new generation of composers. His students, including Pierre Boulez and Karlheinz Stockhausen, were profoundly influenced by his approach to harmony and color. Messiaen's emphasis on the sensory and emotional impact of harmony has left a lasting legacy in contemporary music, inspiring composers to explore new ways of integrating color and sound.

Messiaen's fascination with color was not limited to his music; it also extended to his personal life. He was an avid birdwatcher and nature enthusiast, and his love of the natural world is reflected in his music's vibrant, colorful imagery. In works like "Catalogue d'oiseaux" (Catalogue of Birds), Messiaen combines his synesthetic perceptions with his detailed observations of birdsong, creating a musical portrait of the avian world. The intricate, colorful harmonies in these pieces reflect the rich, diverse sounds of birds, each chord capturing the essence of a different species.

The significance of Messiaen's color chords extends beyond their immediate sensory impact; they also represent a philosophical and spiritual vision. For Messiaen, the experience of color and sound was a way to transcend the material world and glimpse the divine. His music, with its rich, shimmering harmonies, aims to evoke a sense of the infinite and the eternal, inviting listeners to experience a higher, more profound reality.

In conclusion, Olivier Messiaen's synesthesia and his creation of color chords represent one of the most distinctive and innovative aspects of his musical language. His ability to perceive and translate colors into sound allowed him to create music that is both sonically rich and visually evocative. Through his use of color chords, Messiaen expanded the boundaries of harmonic language, creating a unique, multisensory experience that continues to inspire and captivate listeners. His work stands as a testament to the power of synesthesia to enrich and deepen our understanding of music, and to the boundless creativity of one of the 20th century's most visionary composers.

Messiaen's theoretical concepts and his synesthetic experiences were deeply integrated into his compositional practice. His practical application of color chords can be observed in numerous compositions, each demonstrating his mastery of this technique and its profound impact on the overall musical texture.

In "Oiseaux exotiques" (Exotic Birds), Messiaen combines his love of birdsong with his coloristic harmonic language. This piece features a series of bird calls transcribed into piano and orchestral parts, each accompanied by harmonies that reflect the vivid colors Messiaen associated with these sounds.

Another significant example is "Éclairs sur l'au-delà." (Illuminations of the Beyond), one of Messiaen's last works. This orchestral piece, composed in the final years of his life, is a profound exploration of color and light. The music is filled with radiant, shimmering chords that evoke the celestial visions Messiaen often described. These color chords are not merely decorative; they are integral to the piece's structure and emotional impact, guiding the listener through a journey of spiritual illumination.

Messiaen's opera "Saint François d'Assise" is another masterpiece that showcases his use of color chords. The opera's score is filled with harmonies that depict the spiritual experiences of Saint Francis and the natural beauty of the world around him. In the scene where Saint Francis receives the stigmata, Messiaen uses a series of ascending color chords to depict the heavenly light descending upon the saint. This moment, both musically and visually, captures the transcendent essence of Messiaen's artistic vision.

In "Couleurs de la cité céleste" (Colors of the Celestial City), Messiaen's fascination with the Book of Revelation is expressed through a series of color chords that depict the heavenly

Jerusalem. The piece features bright, luminous harmonies that reflect the jewel-like colors described in the biblical text. The music is both awe-inspiring and deeply meditative, drawing the listener into a vision of the divine.

CHAPTER EIGHT

The Teacher's Podium And Nurturing Future Luminaries

Olivier Messiaen's teaching career at the Paris Conservatoire was as influential as his compositional output. Appointed as a professor of harmony in 1941 and later as a professor of composition, Messiaen dedicated over four decades to nurturing and shaping the minds of young composers. His unique approach to music education and his willingness to embrace and encourage innovation made him a beloved and revered figure among his students.

Messiaen's teaching philosophy was deeply rooted in his own experiences as a composer and musician. He believed in the importance of a broad musical education, one that encompassed not only traditional Western classical music but also non-Western musical traditions, bird songs, and the natural world. This holistic approach provided his students with a rich tapestry of musical influences to draw from, encouraging them to think beyond conventional boundaries.

His classes were renowned for their intensity and depth. Messiaen's ability to convey complex musical concepts with clarity and passion made his lectures highly sought after. He emphasized the importance of understanding music theory and harmony, but he also encouraged his students to explore their unique voices and to experiment with new ideas. This balance between technical rigor and creative freedom was a hallmark of Messiaen's teaching.

Messiaen's impact on his students was profound. He cultivated an environment of mutual respect and intellectual curiosity, where students felt free to express their ideas and challenge existing paradigms. His emphasis on the emotional and spiritual aspects of music, combined with his encyclopedic knowledge of musical techniques, provided his students with a comprehensive and inspiring education.

Among Messiaen's many students, Pierre Boulez and Karlheinz Stockhausen stand out as two of the most significant figures in 20th-century music. Both composers were profoundly influenced by Messiaen's teachings, and their work reflects the innovative spirit and deep musical understanding that Messiaen instilled in them.

Pierre Boulez, one of the most influential composers and conductors of the 20th century, studied with Messiaen at the Paris Conservatoire in the early 1940s. Boulez was immediately struck by Messiaen's unique approach to music and his profound understanding of rhythm, harmony, and form. Under Messiaen's guidance, Boulez began to develop his own distinctive musical language, characterized by its complexity and precision.

Messiaen's influence on Boulez can be seen in several key aspects of Boulez's work. First, Messiaen's exploration of rhythm and time deeply affected Boulez's approach to composition. Messiaen introduced Boulez to the idea of treating rhythm as a structural element, rather than merely a decorative one. This led Boulez to experiment with complex rhythmic structures and to develop his own techniques for manipulating time within his compositions.

Second, Messiaen's use of modes of limited transposition and his innovative harmonic language provided Boulez with a new vocabulary for his own music. Boulez adopted and expanded upon these ideas, creating a harmonic language that was both highly original and deeply rooted in Messiaen's teachings. This is particularly evident in Boulez's early works, such as his piano sonatas and his orchestral piece "Le Marteau sans Maître" (The Hammer without a Master).

Third, Messiaen's emphasis on the emotional and spiritual dimensions of music had a lasting impact on Boulez. While Boulez's music is often perceived as highly intellectual and abstract, it is also deeply expressive and charged with a sense of inner intensity. This duality reflects the balance between intellect and emotion that Messiaen fostered in his students.

Boulez's career as a conductor and his advocacy for contemporary music also bear the imprint of Messiaen's influence. Boulez's commitment to performing and promoting new music, as well as his efforts to create institutions like the Institut de Recherche et Coordination Acoustique/Musique (IRCAM) in Paris, echo Messiaen's dedication to musical innovation and education.

Karlheinz Stockhausen, another towering figure in 20th-century music, also studied with Messiaen at the Paris Conservatoire. Stockhausen's time with Messiaen was a pivotal period in his development as a composer. Messiaen's teachings opened Stockhausen's mind to new possibilities in music, inspiring him to explore uncharted territories in sound and composition.

One of the most significant influences Messiaen had on Stockhausen was in the realm of rhythm and time. Messiaen's concepts of non-retrogradable rhythms and rhythmic permutation fascinated Stockhausen and led him to develop his own complex rhythmic techniques. These ideas are evident in Stockhausen's early works, such as "Kontra-Punkte" and "Klavierstücke," where intricate rhythmic structures play a central role.

Messiaen's emphasis on the use of color and timbre in composition also had a profound impact on Stockhausen. Messiaen's exploration of harmonic color and his synesthetic approach to music resonated deeply with Stockhausen, who went on to develop his own theories and practices in this area. Stockhausen's electronic music, in particular, reflects this influence, with its focus on the manipulation of timbre and the creation of rich, multi-layered sonic textures.

Furthermore, Messiaen's openness to non-Western musical traditions and his incorporation of bird songs into his compositions inspired Stockhausen to look beyond the Western classical tradition for his own musical ideas. This led Stockhausen to experiment with a wide range of musical sources, from electronic sounds to world music, and to develop a truly global and eclectic musical language.

Stockhausen's interest in the spiritual and transcendental dimensions of music can also be traced back to Messiaen. Messiaen's deeply held Catholic faith and his belief in music as a means of spiritual expression influenced Stockhausen's own spiritual journey and his exploration of mystical and metaphysical themes in his music.

This is particularly evident in Stockhausen's later works, such as "Licht" and "Inori," which are imbued with a sense of cosmic and spiritual exploration.

Beyond Boulez and Stockhausen, Messiaen's influence extended to a wide range of composers and musicians who studied with him or were inspired by his work. His teachings and his music left an indelible mark on the landscape of contemporary music, shaping the development of new techniques, styles, and ideas.

One of the key aspects of Messiaen's influence was his ability to bridge the gap between tradition and innovation. While deeply rooted in the Western classical tradition, Messiaen was also a tireless explorer of new musical possibilities. This duality made him a compelling and inspiring figure for many young composers who sought to push the boundaries of music while remaining connected to its rich history.

Messiaen's exploration of rhythm, in particular, had a lasting impact on contemporary music. His ideas about rhythmic structure and his use of complex, irregular rhythms opened up new possibilities for composers and performers. This influence can be seen in the works of composers such as Iannis Xenakis, who studied briefly with Messiaen and developed his own highly original rhythmic techniques.

Messiaen's use of modes of limited transposition and his innovative harmonic language also inspired a generation of composers to explore new ways of organizing pitch and harmony. Composers such as Gérard Grisey and Tristan Murail, who were part of the spectral music movement, drew on Messiaen's ideas to develop their own approaches to harmony and timbre.

Messiaen's openness to non-Western musical traditions and his incorporation of bird songs into his compositions also had a profound influence on contemporary music. His willingness to draw on a wide range of musical sources and his emphasis on the natural world as a source of inspiration encouraged many composers to explore new and diverse musical influences. This can be seen in the works of composers such as Toru Takemitsu and George Crumb, who incorporated elements of nature and non-Western music into their own compositions.

Messiaen's legacy as a teacher is a testament to his profound impact on the world of music. His students went on to become some of the most important and influential composers of the 20th century, carrying forward his ideas and innovations while developing their own unique voices. The principles and techniques Messiaen taught continue to resonate in contemporary music, inspiring new generations of composers and musicians.

One of the key aspects of Messiaen's legacy is his emphasis on the importance of personal expression and individuality in music. While he provided his students with a rigorous technical foundation, he also encouraged them to explore their own creative paths and to develop their own distinctive styles. This emphasis on individuality helped to foster a rich diversity of musical voices among his students, each of whom took Messiaen's teachings in unique and innovative directions.

Messiaen's commitment to innovation and experimentation also left a lasting mark on contemporary music. His willingness to explore new musical ideas and to push the boundaries of traditional musical forms inspired his students to do the same. This spirit of innovation is evident in the works of many of his students, who have continued to push the boundaries of music in their own ways.

Furthermore, Messiaen's holistic approach to music education, which encompassed not only Western classical music but also non-Western traditions, bird songs, and the natural world, provided his students with a rich and diverse musical palette to draw from. This broad approach to musical education has had a lasting impact on contemporary music, encouraging composers to explore a wide range of musical influences and to incorporate diverse elements into their own work.

Messiaen's influence also extended beyond his direct students to a wider circle of composers and musicians who were inspired by his music and his ideas. His works, with their rich harmonic language, complex rhythms, and vivid coloristic effects, continue to be performed and studied, inspiring new generations of musicians

Printed in Great Britain
by Amazon